D0418326

Blackbird Singing

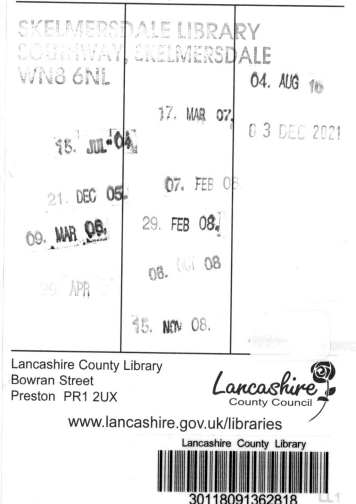

This book should be returned to any branch of the Lancashire County Library on or before the date shown

Lancashire County Library
Bowran Street
Preston PR1 2UX

Lancashire
County Council

www.lancashire.gov.uk/libraries

Blackbird Singing

Poems and Lyrics 1965–1999

PAUL McCARTNEY

Edited and with an Introduction by Adrian Mitchell

faber and faber

First published in 2001
by Faber and Faber Limited
3 Queen Square London WC1N 3AU
This paperback edition first published in 2002

Photoset by Faber and Faber Limited
Printed in England by Mackays of Chatham, plc

0913628l8

Cover drawing by Paul McCartney

A CIP record for this book is available from the British Library

ISBN 0-571-20992-0

10 9 8 7 6 5 4 3 2

to Linda, Mary, Stella, James and Heather

Blackbird

Blackbird singing in the dead of night
Take these broken wings and learn to fly
All your life
You were only waiting for this moment to arise.

Blackbird singing in the dead of night
Take these sunken eyes and learn to see
All your life
You were only waiting for this moment to be free

Blackbird fly
Into the light of a dark black night
Blackbird fly
Into the light of a dark black night

Blackbird singing in the dead of night
Take these broken wings and learn to fly
All your life
You were only waiting for this moment to arise.

Contents

Foreword

When I was a teenager, for some reason I had an overwhelming desire to have a poem published in the school magazine. I wrote something deep and meaningful – which was promptly rejected – and I suppose I have been trying to get my own back ever since.

Years later, after having written many song lyrics with – and without – John Lennon, I wrote a poem on hearing of the death of my dear friend Ivan Vaughan. It seemed to me that a poem, rather than a song, could perhaps best express what I was feeling. This poem 'Ivan' led on to others, many of which are included here.

I was persuaded by Adrian Mitchell that the book should also include song lyrics, which it does, so much so that I now agree with his opinion that both forms of writing have equal capacity to convey great depth of feeling. I hope you, the reader, feel the same.

Paul McCartney

Introduction

In working on this book with Paul, I have chosen the best of Paul's poems and song lyrics. It's been a delight.

I met Paul, John, George, Ringo and Brian way back in January 1963 when the Beatles hit London. I was writing a pop column for the *Daily Mail*, and on 1 February 1963 published the first interview with the group in a national newspaper. I enjoyed meeting them and hearing them play live, and went back to write about them whenever my paper would give me the space. They were a friendly bunch. Paul was interested that I was a published poet and novelist, so I came to know him best.

We maintained a friendship which became closer over the years, especially when our families met. One of the highlights of my life was performing four of my poems backed by Paul, Linda and their band on the Southend leg of his world tour in 1991.

Around that time Linda phoned me to suggest that I edit a collection of Paul's poems. The idea was to keep the project a secret from Paul – it would be a surprise for his birthday. That didn't last long. Paul always knows what's going on around him.

In 1995, when I was poetry editor of the *New Statesman*, I published a page of five of his colourful, impressionist poems – 'Chasing the Cherry', 'Mist the Mind', 'The Blue Shines Through', 'Trouble Is' and 'Velvet Wave'. The sales of that issue of the magazine shot up by several thousand.

We've taken our time in making our selection, partly because Paul had to excavate several crammed tea-chests to find old manuscripts, partly because he's writing some of his best poems now. Sometimes I've made suggestions for small cuts or changes and sometimes Paul's accepted them.

Linda herself had a way with words. She wrote, briefly but poignantly:

Oppression won't win.
The light comes from within.

This book was Linda's idea and she is our inspiration.

Who listens to the words of songs, anyway? I do. And so do millions of people. Plenty of fans painstakingly write down the lyrics of their favourite songs in exercise books.

Of course most songwriters aren't artists of any sort. Mostly they're trying to make money by writing the same words that have made money over and over again. The hit songs of my adolescence in the late 1940s – Crosby, Sinatra, Nat King Cole, Dinah Shore, etc – were full of mushy words like devotion and emotion, plus a few tinselly stars above – awful, empty lyrics, like tons of white mud. But a few funny songs of the time were verbally alive – 'Tallahassee', 'Accentuate the Positive' and the weird 'Cement Mixer'. It was in the blues I found the best words, in gritty numbers like 'Make Me a Pallet on the Floor', 'If You See Me Comin'', 'Saint James Infirmary' and 'Low Down Dirty Shame Blues':

I looked out the window, saw a poor boy walkin' in the rain,
Yeah, looked out the window, saw a poor boy walkin' in the
    rain,
Heard him mutter: 'It's a low down dirty shame.

'I walked the streets all night long, got my feet all soakin' wet,
Walked the streets all night long, feet all soakin' wet,
Ain't seen nobody look like my baby yet –
It's a low down dirty shame.'

That was real true solid gold poetry and I knew it.

It was with rock'n'roll that the dirty truthful words of rhythm and blues broke into radio. Song writers like Chuck Berry and Jerry Leiber wrote story lyrics about city life using images of cars, burgers, love potions, booze, prison riots, strippers, school and trouble of all kinds – fast-moving three-minute poetic dramas. Songs like 'Blue Suede Shoes' and 'Riot in Cell Block Number Nine' were not only delivered like death threats, they were written in the language of reality.

The Beatles loved and sang these songs before they began to grow their own. As their confidence grew, the Lennon/McCartney team shoved back the frontiers of lyric writing to achieve wonders like 'Sergeant Pepper's Lonely Hearts Club Band', 'Come Together', 'Eleanor Rigby' and 'A Day in the Life'. When they parted, John and Paul both kept writing strong and clever lyrics.

Of course the Beatles did far, far more. They changed the world, they opened doors and minds. The Sixties saw a resurgence of the bohemian revolts of Oscar Wilde, Erik Satie, Van Gogh and jazz. But this time many more people joined in. Everybody, it seemed, wanted a bit of it – some freedom, some colour, some poetry, some revolution.

By the late 1950s poetry was changing radically. In the USA a revival of oral poetry was fired by the performances of Dylan Thomas, Allen Ginsberg and others. In Britain, Mike Horovitz first took his Live New Departures circus of poets, musicians, actors and clowns out on the road and continued the good work. Since those ancient days, when almost all published poets seemed to be white male graduates from private schools, more and more barriers have been torn down. Women were the first to demand equal opportunities for their words. Black and Asian poets followed. Gays and even children demanded their rights, claiming that poems can come from anyone. Of course.

The old snobberies still persist – just study the more respectable anthologies and you might still think that poetry is for intellectuals and academics only.

Clean out your head. Wash out the name and the fame. Read these clear words and listen to them – decide for yourself.

Paul is not in the line of academic or modernist poets. He is a popular poet in the tradition of popular poetry. Homer was and is a popular poet, understood and loved by millions of people who never saw a university. William Blake, who used to sing his *Songs of Innocence and Experience* to a small circle of friends, has become one of the most popular of all poets. Whenever critics say there is something inferior about poetry which is sung, my advice is to sing Blake's 'Tyger' or Burns's 'My Luve is like a Red, Red Rose' at them.

A few songwriters, although they know you can get away with banal nothingness in pop lyrics, have a vision and try to convey it to us. A few manage to write truthfully about the world – as Paul does in 'Penny Lane', 'She Came in through the Bathroom Window' and 'Eleanor Rigby'. His best lyrics can well stand alongside Christina Rossetti's 'In the Bleak Midwinter' or Blake's 'A Poison Tree' or Burns's 'This is No My Ain Lassie'.

There's often a difference between a poem and a song lyric. Lyrics tend to be less concentrated, partly because a song has to work instantly, and partly because the words must allow room for the music to breathe, to allow time for the work of the music. In a good song the words and the music dance together, so they need dancing room.

Paul takes risks, again and again, in all of his work. He's not afraid to take on the art of poetry – which is the art of dancing naked. There is a real kinship between Paul's work and poets of today like Brian Patten and Carol Ann Duffy, and also lyric writers like Elvis Costello, Randy Newman and Laurie Anderson.

Paul's not a primitive. He's been writing poems since he was a schoolboy, since the days when his great teacher Alan Durband introduced him to Chaucer and Shakespeare, since his first dis-covery of Oscar Wilde, Tennessee Williams, Bernard Shaw, Sheridan and Hardy. And he has sought advice from living poets as well, friends like Allen Ginsberg and Tom Pickard. Of course Paul is blessed with one of the subtlest, warmest singing voices of our time. Of course his gift for writing tunes which go straight into the heart and stick there is unsurpassed. But he's a jeweller and a juggler when it comes to words. Both his poems and lyrics are full of surprises.

Sometimes his poems are light as feathers. They can tickle or fly or delight the eye. Sometimes he writes four lines as heavy as a double-decker bus, or the heart itself.

To demonstrate the seriousness and sense of Paul's writing, here is his description of how he wrote 'Blackbird', quoted from *Many Years from Now* by Barry Miles:

> I developed the melody on guitar based on the Bach piece and took it somewhere else, took it to another level, then I just fitted the words to it. I had in mind a black woman, rather than a bird. Those were the days of the civil rights movement, which all of us cared passionately about, so this was really a song from me to a black woman, experiencing these problems in the States: 'Let me encourage you to keep trying, to keep your faith, there is hope.'
>
> As is often the case with my things, a veiling took place, so rather than say 'Black woman living in Little Rock' and be very specific, she became a bird, became symbolic, so you could apply it to your particular problem.
>
> This is one of my themes: take a sad song and make it better, let this song help you. 'Empowerment' is a good word for it. Through the years I have had lots of wonderful letters from people saying, 'That song really helped me through a

terrible period.' I think that the single greatest joy of having been a musician, and been in the Beatles, is when those letters come back to you and you find that you've really helped people. That's the magic of it all, that's the wonder, because I wrote them with half an idea that they might help, but it really makes me feel very proud when I realise that they have been of actual help to people.

Not many poets could bear to write as openly and transparently as that about their working methods and their reasons for writing. Paul knows the value of words, how they can help us to enjoy living and loving. He also knows how words can work during the deepest grief – not just as therapy, but as a way of speaking to and for others who have lost their loved ones.

This collection needed no introduction. I wrote one because I wanted to indicate Paul's place in poetry. But these poems and song lyrics stand on their own two feet. Their own two dancing feet. Thank you Paul, thank you Linda.

Adrian Mitchell

1 Playing at Home

In Liverpool

I spent my early life in Liverpool
Something I'm not likely to forget
People blend with places
Faces that I know but never met

Upstairs on a bus behind a man
Talking to himself or so it seemed
Repeating names of old comedians
And laughing at them . . .

Down the pierhead where the preachers met
Each of them his own imagined crowd
Giving us his version of the book
That God had written . . .

In a house before they built the road
Raising jam jars for a worthy cause
Prince the dog with one eye to his name
Wants to follow . . .

By the sports field of the Institute
Lives Soft Sid the harmless village fool
Greeting kids who pass the other side
Saying Hello Children . . .

Listening to the bin man holding court
Promising to buy a brand new bike
King of little children for a day
He gives them money . . .

Walking with the boys of Dungeon Lane
Aimlessly towards a muddy shore
Telling tales about the Chinese farm
And getting captured . . .

I spent my early life in Liverpool
Something I'm not likely to forget
People blend with places
And the faces that I know but never met

In Liverpool.

Mist the Mind

Mist the mind over
With damp's foggy dew
Slide like a tidal wave
Over the rock and
Drowning in merriment
Tell me I am not alone

Hum through the carpet
Nudging the undergrowth
Call out the bad names
To curse every midgy mite
Spin me a reverie
To crack me up

And helpless with laughter
Drop down the mount
A highland waterfall
Searching for love

Figure of Eight

You've got me dancing
In a figure of eight,
Don't know if I'm coming or going,
I'm early or late.
Round and round the ring I go,
I want to know, I want to know,
Why can't we travel a continuous line?
Make love a reliable covenant all the time,
Up and down the hills I go,
I got to know, I got to know.

Is it better to love one another
Than to go for a walk in the dark?
Is it better to love than to give in to hate?
Yeah we'd better take good care of each other
Avoid slipping back off the straight and narrow,
It's better by far than getting stuck
In a figure of eight.

Figure it out for yourself, little girl,
It don't go nowhere at all,
It's nothing more than a tape loop
In a big dance hall.
You've got me running in a figure of eight,
Don't know if I'm coming or going,
I'm early or late,
Round and round that little ring I go,
I want to know, I want to know.

Toy Store

I left for the toy store
I bought myself a whole situation

asking the future for you
wishing the breeze would be mine
chasing the running stream

hoping you'd be tall in the grass

Heart of the Country

I look high, I look low,
I'm lookin' everywhere I go,
Looking for a home
In the heart of the country . . .

I'm gonna move, I'm gonna go,
I'm gonna tell everyone I know,
Looking for a home
In the heart of the country.

Heart of the country
Where the holy people grow,
Heart of the country,
Smell the grass in the meadow.

Want a horse, I want a sheep,
I want to get me a good night's sleep,
Living in a home
In the heart of the country . . .

I'm gonna move, I'm gonna go,
I'm gonna tell everyone I know,
Looking for a home
In the heart of the country.

Mull of Kintyre

Mull of Kintyre
Oh mist rolling in from the sea
My desire is always to be here
Oh Mull of Kintyre

Far have I travelled and much have I seen
Dark distant mountains with valleys of green
Past painted deserts, the sun sets on fire
As he carries me home to the Mull of Kintyre

Sweep through the heather like deer in the glen
Carry me back to the days I knew then
Nights when we sang like a heavenly choir
Of the life and the times of the Mull of Kintyre

Smiles in the sunshine and tears in the rain
Still take me back where my memories remain
Flickering embers grow higher and higher
As they carry me back to the Mull of Kintyre

Mull of Kintyre
Oh mist rolling in from the sea
My desire is always to be here
Oh Mull of Kintyre

When I'm Sixty-Four

When I get older, losing my hair,
    Many years from now,
Will you still be sending me a Valentine,
    Birthday greetings, bottle of wine?
If I've been out till quarter to three
    Would you lock the door?
Will you still need me, will you still feed me
    When I'm sixty-four?

    You'll be older too,
    And if you say the word –
    I could stay with you.

I could be handy, mending a fuse
    When your lights have gone.
You can knit a sweater by the fireside,
    Sunday mornings go for a ride.
Doing the garden, digging the weeds,
    Who could ask for more?
Will you still need me, will you still feed me
    When I'm sixty-four?

    Every summer we can rent a cottage in the Isle of Wight,
    If it's not too dear;
    We shall scrimp and save.
    Grandchildren on your knee –
    Vera, Chuck and Dave.

Send me a postcard, drop me a line,
    Stating point of view,
Indicate precisely what you mean to say,
    Yours sincerely, wasting away.
Give me your answer, fill in a form,
    Mine for evermore.
Will you still need me, will you still feed me
    When I'm sixty-four?

Here Today

(Song for John)

And if I said
I really knew you well
What would your answer be?
If you were here today.

Well, knowing you
You'd probably laugh and say
That we were worlds apart
If you were here today.

But as for me
I still remember how it was before
And I am holding back the tears no more,
I love you.

What about the time we met?
Well I suppose that you could say that
We were playing hard to get,
Didn't understand a thing
But we could always sing.

What about the night we cried?
Because there wasn't any reason left
To keep it all inside,
Never understood a word
But you were always there with a smile.

And if I say I really loved you
And was glad you came along,
Then you were here today
For you were in my song
Here today.

Golden Earth Girl

Golden earth girl, female animal
Sings to the wind, resting at sunset
In a mossy nest
Sensing moonlight in the air
Moonlight in the air.

Good clear-water friend of wilderness
Sees in the pool her own reflection.
In another world
Someone over there is counting.

Fish in a sunbeam,
In eggshell seas.
Fish in a sunbeam,
Eggshell finish.

Nature's lover climbs the primrose hill
Smiles at the sky watching the sunset
From a mossy nest.
As she falls asleep she's counting.

Fish in a sunbeam,
In eggshell seas.
Fish in a sunbeam,
Eggshell
Finish.

Maybe I'm Amazed

Maybe I'm amazed at the way you love me all the time
And maybe I'm afraid of the way I love you,
Maybe I'm amazed at the way you pulled me out of time,
You hung me on a line
Maybe I'm amazed at the way I really need you.

Baby I'm a man
Maybe I'm a lonely man who's in the middle of something
That he doesn't really understand
Baby I'm a man
And maybe you're the only woman who could ever help me,
Baby won't you help me to understand . . .

Maybe I'm amazed at the way you're with me all the time,
Maybe I'm afraid of the way I need you,
Maybe I'm amazed at the way you help me sing my song,
You right me when I'm wrong
And maybe I'm amazed at the way I really need you.

Yellow Submarine

In the town where I was born
Lived a man who sailed to sea,
And he told us of his life
In the land of submarines.

So we sailed off to the sun,
Till we found a sea of green,
And we lived beneath the waves
In our yellow submarine.

   We all live in a yellow submarine,
   Yellow submarine, yellow submarine.

And our friends are all aboard,
Many more of them live next door,
And the band begins to play . . .

   We all live in a yellow submarine,
   Yellow submarine, yellow submarine.

As we live a life of ease,
Every one of us has all we need,
Sky of blue and sea of green,
In our yellow submarine.

   We all live in a yellow submarine,
   Yellow submarine, yellow submarine . . .

Dinner Tickets

My mother always looked
For dinner tickets
In the breast pocket
Of my grey school shirt.

Dried mud
Falls from my workboots.
Zigzag sculptures
Leave a trail as I head
For the woods.

She found a folded drawing
Of a naked woman.
My father asked me about it.

Chainsaw makes easy work
Of young birch blocking my path.

For days I denied all knowledge
Of the shocking work of art.

Resting on a fallen log,
I wipe the sweat from my brow.

Admitting I had made the drawing,
I wept.

Once Upon a Long Ago

Picking up scales and broken chords
Puppy-dog tails in the House of Lords
Tell me darling, what can it mean?

Making up moons in a minor key
What have those tunes got to do with me?
Tell me darling, where have you been?

Once upon a long ago
Children searched for treasure
Nature's plan went hand in hand with pleasure.
Such pleasure

Blowing balloons on a windy day
Desolate dunes with a lot to say
Tell me darling, what have you seen?

Once upon a long ago
Children searched for treasure
Nature's plan went hand in hand
With pleasure.
My pleasure.

Playing guitars on an empty stage
Counting the bars in an iron cage
Tell me darling, what can it mean?

Picking up scales and broken chords
Puppy-dog tails in the House of Lords
Help me darling, what does it mean?

Once upon a long ago . . .

She Came in through the Bathroom Window

She came in through the bathroom window
Protected by a silver spoon
But now she sucks her thumb and wonders
By the banks of her own lagoon.

Didn't anybody tell her?
Didn't anybody see?
Sunday's on the phone to Monday,
Tuesday's on the phone to me.

She said she'd always been a dancer,
She worked at fifteen clubs a day
And though she thought I knew the answer,
Well, I knew but I could not say.

And so I quit the police department
And got myself a steady job
And though she tried her best to help me,
She could steal but she could not rob.

Didn't anybody tell her?
Didn't anybody see?
Sunday's on the phone to Monday,
Tuesday's on the phone to me.

Junk

Motor cars, handlebars, bicycles for two,
Broken-hearted jubilee.
Parachutes, army boots, sleeping bags for two,
Sentimental jamboree.

Buy, buy, says the sign in the shop window.
Why? Why? says the junk in the yard.

Candlesticks, building bricks, something old and new,
Memories for you and me.

Buy, buy, says the sign in the shop window.
Why? Why? says the junk in the yard.

Penny Lane

In Penny Lane there is a barber showing photographs
Of every head he's had the pleasure to know
And all the people that come and go
Stop and say hello.

On the corner is a banker with a motor car,
The little children laugh at him behind his back.
And the banker never wears a mac
In the pouring rain, very strange!

Penny Lane is in my ears and in my eyes.
There beneath the blue suburban skies
I sit and meanwhile back in Penny Lane

There is a fireman with an hour glass
And in his pocket is a portrait of the Queen.
He likes to keep his fire engine clean.
It's a clean machine.

   Penny Lane is in my ears and in my eyes.
   Full of fish-and-finger pies
   In summer, meanwhile back

Behind the shelter in the middle of the roundabout
A pretty nurse is selling poppies from a tray,
And though she feels as if she's in a play
She is anyway.

In Penny Lane the barber shaves another customer,
We see the banker sitting, waiting for a trim.
And then the fireman rushes in from the pouring rain,
Very strange!

Penny Lane is in my ears and in my eyes.
There beneath the blue suburban skies
I sit and meanwhile back . . .
Penny Lane is in my ears and in my eyes,
There beneath the blue suburban skies.
Penny Lane.

(written with John Lennon)

Ivan

Two doors open
On the eighteenth of June
Two babies born
On the same day
In Liverpool
One was Ivan
The other – me
We met in adolescence
And did the deeds
They dared us do
Jive with Ive
The ace on the bass
He introduced to me
At Woolton fete
A pal or two
And so we did
A classic scholar he
A rocking roller me
As firm as friends could be
Cranlock naval
Cranlock pie
A tear is rolling
Down my eye
On the sixteenth of August
Nineteen ninety-three
One door closed
Bye-bye Ivy

The Long and Winding Road

The long and winding road that leads to your door
Will never disappear, I've seen that road before,
It always leads me here, lead me to your door.

The wild and windy night that the rain washed away
Has left a pool of tears crying for the day.
Why leave me standing here?
Let me know the way.

Many times I've been alone and many times I've cried,
Anyway you'll never know the many ways I've tried,
But still they lead me back to the long, winding road,
You left me standing here, a long, long time ago.
Don't leave me waiting here, lead me to your door . . .

The Fool on the Hill

Day after day, alone on a hill,
The man with the foolish grin is keeping perfectly still
But nobody wants to know him,
They can see that he's just a fool
And he never gives an answer.

But the fool on the hill
Sees the sun going down
And the eyes in his head
See the world spinning round.

Well on the way, head in a cloud,
The man of a thousand voices talking perfectly loud
But nobody ever hears him
Or the sound he appears to make
And he never seems to notice.

But the fool on the hill
Sees the sun going down
And the eyes in his head
See the world spinning round.

And nobody seems to like him,
They can tell what he wants to do
And he never shows his feelings.

But the fool on the hill
Sees the sun going down
And the eyes in his head
See the world spinning round.

He never listens to them,
He knows that they're the fools.
They don't like him.

The fool on the hill
Sees the sun going down
And the eyes in his head
See the world spinning round.

This is the Way

(*from* Liverpool Oratorio)

This is the way we put out the candle.
Farewell to childhood.
Deep in the wild wood a fire goes out,
And what are we left with
Now we are grown up?

This is the way we pull up the anchor.
Goodbye to romance.
Out on the ocean a good ship is lost,
And what are we left with
Now we are grown up?

Carry that Weight

Boy, you're gonna carry that weight,
Carry that weight a long time.

I never give you my pillow
I only send you my invitations
And in the middle of the celebrations
I break down.

You never give me your money
You only give me your funny paper
And in the middle of negotiations
You break down.

I never give you my number
I only give you my situation
And in the middle of investigation
I break down.

Boy, you're gonna carry that weight,
Carry that weight a long time.

Hey Jude

Hey Jude, don't make it bad,
Take a sad song and make it better,
Remember to let her into your heart,
Then you can start to make it better.

Hey Jude, don't be afraid,
You were made to go out and get her,
The minute you let her under your skin,
Then you begin to make it better.

   And any time you feel the pain,
   Hey Jude, refrain,
   Don't carry the world upon your shoulders.
   For well you know that it's a fool
   Who plays it cool
   By making his world a little colder.

Hey Jude, don't let me down,
You have found her, now go and get her,
Remember to let her into your heart,
Then you can start to make it better.

   So let it out and let it in,
   Hey Jude, begin,
   You're waiting for someone to perform with.
   And don't you know that it's just you,
   Hey Jude, you'll do,
   The movement you need is on your shoulder.

Hey Jude, don't make it bad,
Take a sad song and make it better,
Remember to let her under your skin,
Then you'll begin to make it better.

Hey Jude . . .

Yesterday

Yesterday
All my troubles seemed so far away,
Now it looks as though they're here to stay,
Oh I believe in
Yesterday.

Suddenly
I'm not half the man I used to be,
There's a shadow hanging over me,
Oh yesterday came
Suddenly.

Why she had to go I don't know,
She wouldn't say.
I said something wrong,
Now I long
For yesterday.

Yesterday
Love was such an easy game to play,
Now I need a place to hide away,
Oh I believe in
Yesterday.

III Friends and Enemies

Let 'Em In

Someone's knockin' at the door
Somebody's ringin' the bell
Someone's knockin' at the door
Somebody's ringin' the bell
Do me a favour, open the door and let 'em in

Sister Suzie, Brother John,
Martin Luther, Phil and Don,
Brother Michael, Auntie Jin,
Open the door and let 'em in . . .

The Poet of Dumbwoman's Lane

(for Spike Milligan)

The voice of the poet
Of Dumbwoman's Lane
Can be heard across
Valleys of sugar-burned cane,
And nostrils that sleep
Through the wildest of nights
Will be twitching to gain
Aromatic insights.

The wife of the farmer
Of Poppinghole Lane
Can be seen from the cab
Of the Robertsbridge train.
And passengers' comments
Frequently turn
To the wages the wife
Of a farmer can earn.
The poet of Dumbwoman's Lane
Sallies forth,
He is hoping for no one to see.

Day with George

(for George Martin)

You have had your white hair cut.
Your son resembles you closely.

Memories slip across
The even landscape.

Gauntlets of close-packed
Road cones,
Heading for the cool zone.

Hearing less, you still make
Plans to set the fiddle flying.
Voice colliding, notions stride
And stream bareback
Towards their home.

Let us eat our meal
Near sunlight
With white polystyrene
Apple juice,
Brown slices,
And small packets of
Butter wrapped in gold.

Fly by Night

You were the one

– they could never reach
– they could never teach

– that always had something
they could never touch

– who wanted so much
– who wanted too much

that nearly had nothing

You were the one

Jerk of All Jerks

I'm a motorist that quite
Likes a drink when he drives
Who causes the loss
Of innocent lives

I'm the guy with the pistol
Who kills your best friend
You can't really blame me
'Cos I'm round the bend

Hello – how are you?
I'm jerk of all jerks
I'm here to undo
All your charitable works
I do it quite simply by
Making mistakes
And one little boo-boo
Is all that it takes
And you're at the mercy of
Jerk of all jerks.

I'm the man that disposes
Of nuclear waste
There's no need to worry
It's perfectly safe.

In fact there is now
Every reason to hope
That if anything happens
I'll easily cope.

Hello – how are you?
I'm jerk of all jerks . . .

I'm the leader who says
As he wages his war
That the children are not
Ones that he's aiming for

Hello.
How are you?
I'm jerk of all jerks . . .

The Note You Never Wrote

Later on, the story goes,
A bottle floated out to sea.
After days, when it had found the perfect spot,
It opened up
And I read the note
That you never wrote to me.

After all, I'm sure you know,
The Mayor of Baltimore is here.
After days now he can finally appear,
Now at last he's here,
But he never is gonna get my vote,
'Cos he never is gonna get a quote
From the little note that you never wrote to me.

Further on, along the line,
I was arrested on the shore,
Holding papers of government galore.
I was taken in,
But I read the note that you never wrote.
Yes I read the note that you never wrote.
Oh I read the note that you never wrote to me.
Me. Me.

Picasso's Last Words (Drink to Me)

A grand old painter died last night,
His paintings on the wall,
Before he went he bade us well,
And said goodnight to us all.

Drink to me, drink to my health,
You know I can't drink any more,
Drink to me, drink to my health,
You know I can't drink any more.

Three o'clock in the morning,
I'm getting ready for bed,
It came without a warning,
But I'll be waiting for you, baby,
I'll be waiting for you there.

So drink to me, drink to my health,
You know I can't drink any more,
Drink to me, drink to my health,
You know I can't drink any more.

49th Fearless Sleep

In empty public waiting room
Remove brown cowboy boots
To walk on glass fragments of
Dolphin ornament that don't cut feet.

White shirt girl writes song,
Poet recognises me and asks about
Donated building.
My son discusses glass piece.

Two red-fleshed newborn babies are adored.
One repeats what I say, ending
With 'Love your mum.'
Poet says 'Call before you leave town.'
What's the number? Doesn't have one.
Never gets calls, but everybody phones.
Search for boots to go,
See miniature kid's pair
Before finding own.

Fond farewells to all.

Masseuse Masseur

Ah so, Japanese masseuse
Lie me on a towel
And work me till I'm loose
Hold my hand
And sing me 'Yesterday'.

Lie, Argentinian masseuse
Beside me on the floor
And work me till I'm loose
Making moaning noises
We'll play girls and boys
Is anyone at home?

Oh you New Orleans masseur
Lie me on a table
And work me till I'm loose
Imagine my leg as hollow bronze
My neck like a giraffe
And I will burn a hole
In your eyes
Till someone comes
To blow the candle out.

Hot as That

As I emerge from a sandy short cut
The lady jogger asks:
How hot is it
In there?

Do you still have that house?
Her male companion asks,
How long do you spend here?

We rent. Three weeks in summer.

A fly flew off a dust dead mouse,
In there.

Do you see a cool man standing before you?
He sweats.
That's how hot it is
In there.

Little Willow

Bend, little willow
Wind's going to blow you
Hard and cold tonight

Life, as it happens
Nobody warns you
Willow, hold on tight

Nothing's gonna shake your love
Take your love away
No one's out to break your heart
It only seems that way . . . Hey

Sleep, little willow
Peace gonna follow
Time will heal your wounds

Grow to the heavens
Now and forever
Always came too soon

Little willow

Nothing's gonna shake your love
Take your love away
No one's out to break your heart
It only seems that way . . . Hey

Bend little willow
Wind's gonna blow you
Hard and cold tonight

Life, as it happens
Nobody warns you
Willow, hold on tight

Ah, little willow

Little willow

IV The Business

Band on the Run

Stuck inside these four walls
Sent inside forever
Never seeing no one nice again
Like you, mama, you, mama, you

If I ever get out of here
Thought of giving it all away
To a registered charity
All I need is a pint a day if I ever get out of here
(If we ever get out of here)

Well, the rain exploded with a mighty crash
As we fell into the sun
And the first one said to the second one there
I hope you're having fun

Band on the run, band on the run
And the jailer man and Sailor Sam
Were searching everyone
For the band on the run, band on the run
Band on the run, band on the run.

Well, the undertaker drew a heavy sigh
Seeing no one else had come
And a bell was ringing in the village square
For the rabbits on the run

Well the night was falling as the desert world
Began to settle down
In the town they're searching for us everywhere
But we never will be found

Band on the run, band on the run
And the county judge who held a grudge
Will search for evermore
For the band on the run . . .

Spirit of Rock 'n' Roll

Hey alligator
When the school bell rings
Gonna see you later
Around the corner
Walking your crocodile

Miss Information
When the train pulls in
To the railway station
I'll be waiting for you
Wearing such a silly grin

Back in the USSR

Flew in from Miami Beach BOAC,
Didn't get to bed last night.
On the way the paper bag was on my knee,
Man I had a dreadful flight.

    I'm back in the USSR
    You don't know how lucky you are, boy
    Back in the USSR.

Been away so long I hardly knew the place,
Gee it's good to be back home.
Leave it till tomorrow to unpack my case.
Honey, disconnect the phone.

    I'm back in the USSR
    You don't know how lucky you are, boy
    Back in the US back in the US
    Back in the USSR.

Well the Ukraine girls really knock me out,
They leave the West behind.
And Moscow girls make me sing and shout
That Georgia's always on my mind.

    I'm back in the USSR

Show me round your snow-peaked mountains way down
         south,
Take me to your daddy's farm,
Let me hear your balalaikas ringing out,
Come and keep your comrade warm.

   I'm back in the USSR
   You don't know how lucky you are, boy
   Back in the USSR.

Backwards Traveller

Hey, did you know that I'm
Always going back in time
Rhyming slang, auld lang syne my dears
Through the years

I am the backwards traveller
Ancient wool unraveller
Sailing songs, wailing on the moon

And we were sailing songs, wailing on the moon
Wailing on the moon

Velvet Wave

The velvet inside
A guitar case
Set the strings
Giddy humming to
The silver vibration of a note

A quick flowing
Stream by the roadside
Buzzed towards the seaside
Tattoos and Torture Tents
Along the shingle shore

Thin echoes of headphones
Ride the murky old bass
Screaming feedback
At the fat lady bather

A wave flaps in on itself

Why Don't We Do It in the Road?

Why don't we do it in the road?
Why don't we do it in the road?
No one will be watching us.
Why don't we do it in the road?

Why don't we do it in the road?
Why don't we do it in the road?
No one will be watching us.
Why don't we do it in the road?

Why don't we do it in the road?
Why don't we do it in the road?
No one will be watching us.
Why don't we do it in the road?

Helen Wheels

Said farewell to my last hotel,
It never was much kind of abode,
Glasgow town never brought me down
When I was heading out on the road.
Carlisle city never looked so pretty,
And the Kendal freeway's fast,
Slow down driver, want to stay alive,
I want to make this journey last.

  Helen, hell on wheels
  Ain't nobody else gonna
  Know the way she feels
  Helen, hell on wheels
  And they never gonna
  Take her away.

M6 south down to Liverpool,
Where they play the West Coast sound,
Sailor Sam he came from Birmingham,
But he never will be found.
Doing fine when a London sign
Greets me like a long lost friend,
Mister Motor, won't you check her out,
She's got to take me back again.

  Helen, hell on wheels . . .

Got no time for a rum and lime,
I wanna get my right foot down,
Shake some dust off of this old bus,
I gotta get her out of town.
Spend the day upon the motorway
Where the carburettors blast,
Slow down driver, want to stay alive,
I want to make this journey last.

    Helen, hell on wheels
    Ain't nobody else gonna
    Know the way she feels
    Helen, hell on wheels
    And they never gonna
    Take her away.

Monkberry Moon Delight

So I sat in the attic
A piano up my nose
And the wind played a dreadful cantata
Sore was I from the crack
Of an enemy's hose
And the horrible sound of tomato

    Ketchup soup and purée
    Don't get left behind . . .

    Ketchup soup and purée
    Don't get left behind . . .

When a rattle of rats had awoken
The sinews, the nerves and the veins
My piano is boldly outspoken
And attempts to repeat his refrain
So I stood with a knot in my stomach
Then I gazed at the terrible sight
Of two youngsters concealed in a barrel
Sucking Monkberry Moon Delight

    Monkberry Moon Delight . . .
    Monkberry Moon Delight . . .
    Monkberry Moon Delight . . .
    Monkberry Moon Delight . . .

Well I know my banana
Is older than the rest
And my hair is a tangled beretta
Well I leave my pyjamas
To Billy Budapest
And I don't get the gist of your letter

    Catch up
    Cats and kittens
    Don't get left behind . . .

    Catch up
    Cats and kittens
    Don't get left behind . . .

    Monkberry Moon Delight . . .
    Monkberry Moon Delight . . .

    Monkberry Moon Delight . . .
    Monkberry Moon Delight . . .
    Monkberry Moon Delight . . .
    Monkberry Moon Delight . . .

Sucking Monkberry Moon Delight . . .

(written with Linda McCartney)

Black Vulcan

Did you ever see a dog so strong and fast
He's the only one that's never been last
Black Vulcan
Oh Black Vulcan

He ain't no ord-in-ary pup,
He's eight feet tall when he stands up
Black Vulcan
Oh Black Vulcan

Moo-oove Black Vulcan
Moo-oove Black Vulcan
You've gotta go
Got all my dough
On you
Yes, yes

Moo-oove Black Vulcan
Moo-oove Black Vulcan
You've gotta go
Got all my dough
On you!

Venus and Mars

Sitting in the stand of the sports arena,
Waiting for the show to begin.
Red lights, green lights, strawberry wine,
A good friend of mine follows the stars,
Venus and Mars are alright tonight.

Reprise

Standing in the hall of the great cathedral,
Waiting for the transport to come.
Starship 21ZNA9 a good friend of mine studies the stars,
Venus and Mars are alright tonight.

Come away on a strange vacation, holiday hardly begun.
Run into a good friend of mine,
Sold me a sign, reach for the stars,
Venus and Mars are alright tonight.
   Ah. Ah. Ah. Ah.

Sergeant Pepper's Lonely Hearts Club Band

It was twenty years ago today
That Sergeant Pepper taught the band to play.
They've been going in and out of style
But they're guaranteed to raise a smile.
So may I introduce to you
The act you've known for all these years –
Sergeant Pepper's Lonely Hearts Club Band!

We're Sergeant Pepper's Lonely Hearts Club Band,
We hope you will enjoy the show.
We're Sergeant Pepper's Lonely Hearts Club Band,
Sit back and let the evening go.
Sergeant Pepper's Lonely, Sergeant Pepper's Lonely,
Sergeant Pepper's Lonely Hearts Club Band.

It's wonderful to be here,
It's certainly a thrill.
You're such a lovely audience,
We'd like to take you home with us,
We'd love to take you home.

I don't really want to stop the show,
But I thought you might like to know,
That the singer's going to sing a song,
And he wants you all to sing along.

So let me introduce to you
The one and only Billy Shears
And Sergeant Pepper's Lonely Hearts Club Band ...

The Song We Were Singing

For a while we could sit, smoke a pipe
And discuss all the vast intricacies of life
We could jaw through the night
Talk about a range of subjects, anything you like
Oh yeah.

But we always came back to the song we were singing
At any particular time,
Yeah we always came back to the song we were singing
At any particular time.

Take a sip, see the world through a glass
And speculate about the cosmic solution
To the sound, blue guitars
Caught up in a philosophical discussion,
Oh yeah.

But we always came back to the song we were singing.

v The World Tonight

The World Tonight

I saw you sitting at the centre of a circle
Everybody, everybody wanted something from you
I saw you sitting there

I saw you swaying to the rhythm of your music
Caught you playing, caught you praying to the voice inside you
I saw you swaying there

I don't care what you want to be
I go back so far I'm in front of me!
It doesn't matter what they say
They're giving the game away

I can see the world tonight
Look into the future
See it in a different light
I can see the world tonight

I heard you listening to a secret conversation
You were crying, you were trying not to let them hear you
I heard you listening in

Never mind what they want to do
You've got a right to your point of view!
It doesn't matter what they say
They're giving the game away
I can see the world tonight

I saw you hiding from a flock of paparazzi
You were hoping, you were hoping that the ground would swallow you
I saw you hiding there

I don't care what you want to be
I go back so far I'm in front of me!
It doesn't matter what they say
They're giving the game away

I can see the world tonight
Look into the future
See it in a different light
I can see the world tonight

Chasing the Cherry

Fragile fragments
Clattering down
The lavish marble staircase
Tinkling smithereens
Smashing, grabbing
At china stars
Bursting in clusters,
Scattering E-side cats
Credit cards dropping
From rain-clouds
Pour down on the well-polished floor
Tortoiseshell hair-combs
And black tape cassettes
Rattle the cages of
Knife-wielding grand dames

And say, are you chasing the cherry?
The merry-go-round of the roses
If so, you must know
That the downside
Is to sink like a ferry

Ascending the slope
In herring-bone fashion
Holding on chromium steel
Lifting the bar bells
With candlestick motion
Side-stepping hot wax,
And wheel

Flying with lizards
All blown in a gust
Through staining glass
Windows and covered with dust blood,
To keep out the rain

And say, are you chasing the cherry?
The merry-go-round of the roses
If so, you must know
That the down side
Is to sink like a ferry

A weapon is not
Worth a button,
When anti-world
Matters explode
And chandeliers
Drop from the ceiling
With sharp-shooters' skill

Exhausted collapse
In the playground
Apeak epileptic remains
And froth at the mouth
Like a river, till
Teachers in apple-pie beds
Reach out
Chalk filled hands
And lift
Lift

And say, are you chasing the cherry?
The singular red one on top
It gleams with particular pleasure
That may never stop
If so, you must know
That the high tide
Has sunk like a ferry.

Was It Really Twenty Years Ago?

What's changed?
Issues still the same

Then we wanted

END APARTHEID
PEACE ON EARTH
LOVE & UNDERSTANDING

Now
What have we learned?

CHANGE COMES SLOWLY
But it is
CHANGING!!!

   KEEP PUSHING

KEEP THE FAITH
   AND PRAY
THAT WE HAVE BETTER NEWS TO REPORT

TWENTY YEARS FROM TODAY

Big Boys Bickering

Big boys bickering,
That's what they're doing every day.
Big boys bickering,
Fucking it up for everyone.

Guess why they're betting on the track?
They're trying to win your money back.
All of the taxes that you paid
Went to fund a masquerade.

Big boys bickering ...

We stand here waiting
Underneath the tower block,
Who will win, who will lose?
Which way do the big boys choose?
Which of us will ever know
What goes on?

So while they argue through the night,
Shaking their sticks of dynamite,
Babies are dying through the day,
They want to blow us all away.

Big boys bickering
And so the game goes on and on.
Big boys bickering,
Fucking it up for everyone.
For everyone!

City Park

Twenty-seven press-ups
At black park bench altar.
Eight warm even notes
From tall church cool bell.
High staccato twittering of small birds
Against throbbing pigeons
'Oh how do you do?
Oh how do you coo?'

World's long low surface
Tickles to life with strangers,
Sniffing collie couple,
Speed-walking high-armed
Brisk little sergeant major woman.
Bouncing peke in tow.

Moorhen flutters squawking
Cross crowded city pond top,
All sorts of ducks,
Mill slowly round white swans.
Stately black swans
Snow tipped nipple red beaks.

A crow cackles
With thumb on black comb rasp.

Winter-bare rose bushes
Line asphalt path.
Old yellow Scotch,
Pink Posy, Pour Toi,
Polar Star, Mood Music
And Yesterday.
Where silent gardeners dig.

Eighteen press-ups
Facing my lover's home
Grins to the sky.
Nine nods this way
Nine nods that.
And I pray
To the spirit of goodness
To open page on a fine, fine day
For ever, and ever,
And EVER
And EVER!

Moon's a Mandarin

Moon's a mandarin
Orange segment.
Stars as clear as you like.
Smelling of pines
And eucalyptus.

Quite a night.

Trouble Is

Rabbit running in circles
chasing his tail because
it looks like candy floss.
Trouble is – rabbits don't eat candy floss.

Black labrador barking at the antics
of his shadow on the wall.
Trouble is – shadows don't fight back.

A pair of gloves hanging from
a back pocket argue about
which hand will hold the rake.
Trouble is – gloves don't give a shit.

A Billion Bees in the Borage

And if, instead of passing,
You stop,
You can hear the hum.
Billions of them
Bobbing from star to star.
Though flowers
Are sky blue, from a
Distance the field looks purple.
Each bee is different
And as they roam
The borage field
They hum.

Give the Man a Break

Workers on the picket line
picking up the trash
executive negotiators
shout about the cash

Workers on the inside
whipping up the dough
while the old man's country
gets to go too slow

   go-go-go

Give the man a break
give the guy a chance
ain't no law say a man can't dance

Doctors gonna operate
wants to know if you'd
like to buy a kidney
mustn't eat the food

Later in the hospital
while he's on the job
poisoned in the kitchen
by a dirty slob

Give the man a break
give the guy a chance
ain't no law say a man can't dance . . .

Looking for Changes

I saw a cat with a machine in his brain
The man who fed him said
He didn't feel any pain
I'd like to see that man
Take out that machine
And stick it in his own brain
You know what I mean

I saw a rabbit with its eyes full of tears
The lab that owned her had
Been doing it for years
Why don't we make them
Pay for every last eye
That couldn't cry its own tears
Do you know what I mean

Well I tell you that we'll all be
Looking for changes
Changes in the way
We treat our fellow creatures
And we will learn how to grow
When we're looking for changes

I saw a monkey that was
Learning·how to choke
A guy beside him gave him
Cigarettes to smoke
And every time that monkey
Started to cough
The bastard laughed his head off
Do you know what I mean

When I tell you that we'll all be
Looking for changes
Changes in the way
We treat our fellow creatures
And we will learn how to grow
When we're looking for changes
We're looking for changes
In the way we are

All Together Now

One, two, three, four,
Can I have a little more?
Five, six, seven, eight, nine, ten,
I love you.

A, B, C, D,
Can I bring my friend to tea?
E, F, G, H, I, J,
I love you.

Bom bom bom bom bom-pa bom
Sail the ship bom-pa bom
Chop the tree bom-pa bom
Skip the rope bom-pa bom
Look at me.

All together now. All together now.

Black, white, green, red,
Can I take my friend to bed?
Pink, brown, yellow, orange and blue,
I love you.

Bom bom bom bom bom-pa bom
Sail the ship bom-pa bom
Chop the tree bom-pa bom
Skip the rope bom-pa bom
Look at me.

All together now!
All together NOW!

She's Leaving Home

Wednesday morning at five o'clock as the day begins,
Silently closing her bedroom door,
Leaving the note that she hoped would say more,
She goes downstairs to the kitchen
Clutching her handkerchief,
Quietly turning the back door key,
Stepping outside, she is free.

She (*We gave her most of our lives*)
Is leaving (*Sacrificed most of our lives*)
Home (*We gave her everything money could buy*).
She's leaving home after living alone
For so many years.
Bye, bye.

Father snores as his wife gets into her dressing gown,
Picks up the letter that's lying there.
Standing alone at the top of the stairs
She breaks down and cries to her husband,
Daddy, our baby's gone.
Why would she treat us so thoughtlessly?
How could she do this to me?

She (*We never thought of ourselves*)
Is leaving (*Never a thought for ourselves*)
Home (*We struggled hard all our lives to get by*).
She's leaving home after living alone
For so many years.
Bye, bye.

Friday morning at nine o'clock she is far away,
Waiting to keep the appointment she made,
Meeting a man from the motor trade.
She (*What did we do that was wrong?*)
Is having (*We didn't know it was wrong*)
Fun (*Fun is the one thing that money can't buy*).
Something inside that was always denied
For so many years.

She's leaving home
Bye, bye.

(written with John Lennon)

Lady Madonna

Lady Madonna, children at your feet
Wonder how you manage to make ends meet.
Who finds the money when you pay the rent?
Did you think that money was heaven sent?

Friday night arrives without a suitcase
Sunday morning creeping like a nun
Monday's child has learned to tie his bootlace.
See how they run.

Lady Madonna, baby at your breast
Wonders how you manage to feed the rest.

Lady Madonna, lying on the bed
Listen to the music playing in your head.

Tuesday afternoon is never ending
Wednesday morning papers didn't come
Thursday night your stockings needed mending.
See how they run.

Lady Madonna, children at your feet
Wonder how you manage to make ends meet.

'Soily

People gathered here tonight,
I want you to listen to me!
To your left and to your right,
You've got some pretty soily company.
Readers, writers, farmer, priest,
Breed-controller, born deceased.
Indian, lawyer, doctor, dog,
And a plumber with a fattened hog.

'Soily, 'soily,
The cat in the satin trousers said it's oily.
'Soily, 'soily,
The cat in the satin trousers said it's oily,
And you know he's right.

Romans, Italians, countrymen,
I want you to listen to me !
I've said it twice and I'll say it again,
We've got some pretty soily company.
Liar, cheater, jungle chief,
Saint, believer on relief.
Action painter, Hitler's son,
And a commie with a tommy gun.

'Soily, 'soily,
The cat in the satin trousers said it's oily.
'Soily, 'soily,
The cat in the satin trousers said it's oily,
And you know he's right.

Maxwell's Silver Hammer

Joan was quizzical, studied pataphysical
Science in the home,
Late nights all alone with a test-tube,
Oh oh oh oh.
Maxwell Edison majoring in medicine
Calls her on the phone,
Can I take you out to the pictures, Joan?
But as she's getting ready to go,
A knock comes on the door.

    Bang bang Maxwell's silver hammer
    Came down upon her head.
    Bang bang Maxwell's silver hammer
    Made sure that she was dead.

Back in school again, Maxwell plays the fool again,
Teacher gets annoyed.
Wishing to avoid an unpleasant scene,
She tells Max to stay when the class has gone away,
So he waits behind,
Writing fifty times I must not be so oh oh oh.
But when she turns her back on the boy
He creeps up from behind.

    Bang bang Maxwell's silver hammer
    Came down upon her head.
    Bang bang Maxwell's silver hammer
    Made sure that she was dead.

PC Thirty-One said, We've caught a dirty one,
Maxwell stands alone
Painting testimonial pictures
Oh oh oh oh.
Rose and Valerie screaming from the gallery
Say he must go free.
The Judge does not agree and he tells them so oh oh oh.
But as the words are leaving his lips
A noise comes from behind.

    Bang bang Maxwell's silver hammer
    Came down upon his head.
    Bang bang Maxwell's silver hammer
    Made sure that he was dead.
      Silver hammer man.

Paperback Writer

Dear Sir or Madam will you read my book?
It took me years to write, will you take a look?
It's based on a novel by a man named Lear,
And I need a job,
So I want to be a
Paperback writer, paperback writer.

It's a dirty story of a dirty man
And his clinging wife doesn't understand.
His son is working for the *Daily Mail*,
It's a steady job,
But he wants to be a
Paperback writer.

It's a thousand pages give or take a few,
I'll be writing more in a week or two.
I can make it longer if you like the style,
I can change it round
And I want to be a
Paperback writer, paperback writer.

If you really like it you can have the rights,
It could make a million for you overnight.
If you must return it you can send it here,
But I need a break
And I want to be a
Paperback writer, paperback writer.

Not On

Take your hand off my knee, young man,
Said the lady in green
I don't care to come between
You and your young woman

It's just not done!

Couldn't we pass up?
Couldn't we fold?
Aren't certain stories
Best left untold?
Some things like
Buttons
Are best left undone

– It's not on!

Arnie Pipe was a normal type
With an average job
Though his prospects will never be great
His bosses underestimate
His value
(Arnie says).

Irene's his fiancée
And would hate to disagree
But the company she thinks is fair
Arnie never does get anywhere
The company owns his underwear
(Clean and well paid for).

Take your feet off my desk, young man,
Said the chauffeur in grey
My green woman has been to see me
She's retreating from your advance –

It just isn't done!

Couldn't you join us?
When can you start
Up as a driver
Looking the part?

Hang on says Arnie –

Couldn't we pass up?
Couldn't we fold?
Aren't certain stories
Best left untold?
Some things like
Buttons
Are best left undone

– It's not on!

Rocky Raccoon

Now somewhere in the black mountain hills of Dakota
There lived a young boy called Rocky Raccoon.
And one day his woman ran off with another guy,
Hit young Rocky in the eye, Rocky didn't like that.
He said, I'm gonna get that boy.
So one day he walked into town,
Booked himself a room in the local saloon.

Rocky Raccoon checked into his room
Only to find Gideon's Bible.
Rocky had come equipped with a gun
To shoot off the legs of his rival.

His rival, it seems, had broken his dreams
By stealing the girl of his fancy.
Her name was Magill and she called herself Lill,
But everyone knew her as Nancy.

Now she and her man who called himself Dan
Were in the next room at the hoe-down.
Rocky burst in and grinning a grin
He said, Danny boy, this is a showdown.

But Daniel was hot – he drew first and shot
And Rocky collapsed in the corner.
Now the doctor came in, stinking of gin
And proceeded to lie on the table.

He said, Rocky you met your match.
And Rocky said, Doc it's only a scratch
And I'll be better, I'll be better Doc
As soon as I'm able.

Now Rocky Raccoon he fell back in his room
Only to find Gideon's Bible.
Gideon checked out and he left it no doubt
To help with good Rocky's revival.

Lovely Rita

Lovely Rita, meter maid,
Nothing can come between us,
When it gets dark I tow your heart away.

Standing by a parking meter,
When I caught a glimpse of Rita,
Filling in a ticket in her little white book.

In a cap she looked much older
And the bag across her shoulder
Made her look a little like a military man.

Lovely Rita, meter maid,
May I inquire discreetly,
When are you free
To take some tea with me?

Took her out and tried to win her,
Had a laugh and over dinner,
Told her I would really like to see her again.

Got the bill and Rita paid it,
Took her home and nearly made it,
Sitting on a sofa with a sister or two.

O, lovely Rita, meter maid,
Where would I be without you?
Give us a wink and make me think of you.

Tchaico

I knew Tchaikovsky
He lived round our way
He was dead good at music
    They used to say
        I called him
Tchaico the Psycho

Junior's Farm

You should have seen me with the poker man
I had a honey and I bet a grand
Just in the nick of time I looked at his hand
I was talking to an Eskimo
Said he was hoping for a fall of snow
When up popped a sea lion ready to go

Let's go, let's go, let's go, let's go
Down to Junior's Farm where I wanna lay low
Low life, high life, oh let's go
Take me down to Junior's Farm

At the Houses of Parliament
Everybody's talking about the President
We all chip in for a bag of cement
Ollie Hardy should have had more sense
He bought a gee-gee and he jumped the fence
All for the sake of a couple of pence

Let's go, let's go, let's go, let's go
Down to Junior's Farm where I wanna lay low
Low life, high life, oh let's go
Take me down to Junior's Farm
Everybody tag along

I took my bag into a grocer's store
The price is higher than the time before
Old man asked me, Why is it more?
I said, You should have seen me with the poker man
I had a honey and I bet a grand.
Just in the nick of time I looked at his hand

Let's go, let's go, let's go, let's go
Down to Junior's Farm where I wanna lay low
Low life, high life, oh let's go
Take me down to Junior's Farm

Take me back, take me back
I wanna go there . . .

Ob-la-di, Ob-la-da

Desmond has a barrow in the market place.
Molly is the singer in a band.
Desmond says to Molly, Girl I like your face
And Molly says this as she takes him by the hand.

Ob-la-di ob-la-da life goes on, bra,
Lala how the life goes on.

Desmond takes a trolley to the jeweller's store,
Buys a twenty-carat diamond ring.
Takes it back to Molly waiting at the door
And as he gives it to her she begins to sing.

Ob-la-di ob-la-da life goes on, bra,
Lala how the life goes on.

In a couple of years they have built
A home sweet home,
With a couple of kids running in the yard
Of Desmond and Molly Jones.

Happy ever after in the market place,
Desmond lets the children lend a hand.
Molly stays at home and does her pretty face
And in the evening she still sings it with the band.

Happy ever after in the market place,
Molly lets the children lend a hand.
Desmond stays at home and does his pretty face
And in the evening she's a singer with the band.

And if you want some fun –
Take Ob-la-di Ob-la-da.

Wedding Invitation

I was told by an American woman
Who was busy looking fixing me a drink
That the children in the building drove her crazy
She may be leaving sooner than you think

Well I said that that was pretty high and mighty
She showed a devastating sense of style
When she replied, 'It was the fault of automation
That I forgot to have a child.'

   Waiting for a wedding invitation
   Thinking one was going to come along
   What you don't know won't hurt you . . .

The bride was looking bitter in a white dress.
The wedding guests had started to arrive.
She said, 'My future husband doesn't understand me
But he's glad to be alive.'

The groom had been a scientific genius
He invented something falling out of bed
But the whole thing nearly turned into a nightmare
When a dirty-looking priest pronounced him dead.

   He said I'm waiting for a wedding invitation
   Thinking one is going to come along
   What you don't know won't hurt you

        I'm not putting you down
    I will walk with you anywhere you want to go
        I'm not putting you down
    I will help you with anything you want to know

While working on a piece of apparatus
He discovered that the world was in a mess
So she made him up a sandwich in the kitchen
And let good old Mother Nature do the rest . . .

It's a handed-down American tradition
A prejudice that still exists today
If it wasn't for their openness of spirit
They might have long ago been spirited away.

    They're waiting for a wedding invitation
    Thinking one is going to come along
    What they don't know won't hurt them

        I'm not putting you down
    I will walk with you anywhere you want to go
        I'm not putting you down
    I will help you with anything you want to know

I'm waiting for a wedding invitation
Thinking one is going to come along
What I don't know won't hurt me . . .

Flaming Pie

Making love underneath the bed
Shooting stars from a purple sky
I don't care how I do it
I'm the man on the flaming pie

Stick my tongue out and lick my nose
Tuck my shirt in and zip my fly
Go ahead, have a vision
I'm the man on the flaming pie

Everything I do has a simple explanation
When I'm with you, you could do with a vacation
I took my brains out and stretched 'em on the rack
Now I'm not so sure I'm ever gonna get 'em back

Cut my toes off to spite my feet
I don't know whether to laugh or cry
Never mind, check my rhythm
I'm the man on the flaming pie

I'm the man on the flaming pie
Now everything I do has a simple explanation
When I'm with you, you could do with a vacation
I took my brains out and stretched 'em on the rack
Now I'm not so sure I'm ever gonna get 'em back

Eleanor Rigby

Ah, look at all the lonely people.
Ah, look at all the lonely people.

  Eleanor Rigby
Picks up the rice in the church where a wedding has been,
  Lives in a dream.
  Waits at the window,
Wearing the face that she keeps in a jar by the door,
  Who is it for?

All the lonely people, where do they all come from?
All the lonely people, where do they all belong?

  Father Mackenzie,
Writing the words of a sermon that no one will hear,
  No one comes near.
  Look at him working,
Darning his socks in the night when there's nobody there,
  What does he care?

All the lonely people, where do they all come from?
All the lonely people, where do they all belong?

  Eleanor Rigby
Died in the church and was buried along with her name.
  Nobody came.
  Father Mackenzie,
Wiping the dirt from his hands as he walks from the grave.
  No one was saved.

All the lonely people, where do they all come from?
All the lonely people, where do they all belong?

VII Standing Stone

Standing Stone

I

After heavy light years
of tenacious trajectory
a ball of fire spat through space
spitting sparks and flames
at new blue universe.

The rains came and came
and extinguished livid flames.
A resistant hiss.
Brooding underground,
a sullen skulking sulk.

Still air hung still.
Silent peaks draped with mist.
A rumbling distance, flash-lit
rain-soaked slopes; valleys
filled with long quiet lakes.
Still air hung still.

Soothed land lay damp.
Reflecting water skimmed the blue
it was hurled through.
Down low toes of ocean rock
streams of lava froze in shock,
arms locked
round stone lover.

Wept sky swept and grey.
A rainbow bridge
cuts mountain tops.

Souped in pea green
a single cell bulb flicked
to life.

Cell burst,
a shot blot page on time,
and grew to be
all living things.

II

He awoke startled
in sparkling imperfection.
Tingling delights of air's fresh rush
collide with grey cloud solitude.
On desolate hazy morning shore
the first person singular wanted
he didn't know what.

Clapping flash of lightning
illuminates far flat lines.
Velvet wind on dark horizon.
Sea of glass.
Then there was melody
made like a memory. A sprinkling of bells.
He sought the source.

Salt sea-breezes quickened,
a shift of silver lifted mist.
A crystal ship slipped and shone in sunlight.
Seduced he swam
to stand on deck.
Wind spoke
and sucked the boat to sea.
Soon land was left
bow fell on swells:
narcotic memory,
untroubled troughs.

A withering wind scratched the deck.
Shivering elegance slivered in splinters,
dissolved in dark as sun spat out.
Breathless lament in dissonant air,
chasms cough up chasms,
spinning wheels of fog.
Hope so hard to float it sank.

Until a crack of blinding light broke through
and hauled the boat along a singing slipway,
towards a dear blue sky.
And as before clear music led the way.

White bird silence over crystal bow.
The vessel sped through beads of spray
that slapped his happy face; and filled his soul
with glory song.
His nostrils snorted blasts of ocean air.
'In thanks for my survival
I'll put up a monument of stone
where I put in.'

III

Subtle colours merged soft contours
stretched in welcome as the ship drew near.
His first bare step on mustard sand
was wiped by whim of wave.

Flickering birdsong.
A bank of grassy moorland rose to distant ridge.
Ancient olive, bright young lime,
and further purple mountain peaks
breathed echoes of the melody.

He stalked through swelling heather
to the ridge's tip to sip
the fresh world's news.
Flanked by juniper and birch
a long-flung track strung out below,
and wound to smoky settlement,
nested in blue hills.

Two natives drove a flock of umber sheep
along this burnt sienna road.
A beautiful woman, from whose throat
the haunting song had come.
A bearded man with snowish hair, her father,
who had witnessed his arrival in a ship of glass
that disappeared as fast as it had come.
These companions walked within his joy
towards the settlement and spoke
of how they'd long expected him.

Still as stones that lined their path

this shepherd's daughter listened to his story.
Her father sang of local life and introduced
each character and scene.
Farmer, warrior, milkmaid, thief,
shaman, housewife, woodsman, fool.
They made him welcome and, before he slept,
agreed to help him hoist his stone.

On sun-smacked days they traced his steps
to plant a giant slab of sea-beat rock.
Rope and muscle, sweat and tackle
raised a weathered finger to the sky.
Soon this sacred stone bedded in its depths
the aspirations of their anxious souls.
A place of peace where he and she would meet.

But as their hearts rehearsed and played a set
of new-found harmonies and chords,
black horse rider rode throughout the night
with news that set the settlement alight.
Off ragged Northern coast
a rugged gang of bandits gathered.
Dark longships flashed with metal.
Thud of boot, belt, hull and oar,
a storm of fighters swarmed ashore.

Panic scampered through the people's veins.
Poisoned rats in a pot of grain.
The visitor fell still to seek an answer.
The shepherdess, his love,
took him
to the standing stone
and poured an ancient potion.

A backward somersault of senses.
Cool breezes
        fruit blossom fragrance rippled air
chiming towers ran slow hours,
        fluttering calm.
And drifted, drifted.
Long spiralled colours twisted
sinuous dance of snake and vine.
She left him to his slab of stone.

He watched its towered rush
scratch at the moon.
Fanned flames flicked up tongues.
Lichen crawled with lunar cloud reflections.
As raging hordes rode tidal waves of blood
he was tossed and smackly landed
on the sudden floor.

He looked up and saw
a spirit force stretch easy into space
so powerful he trembled and believed.
Head bowed, he slipped in trance-wet sheets.
Slow whirl, silent thunder,
breezeless hurricane. He cried out.
A wall of peeled-back veils revealed
a face unlike another.
Vision, visage, gentle, genteel,
masculine mouth, female eyes.
A face to steal.
The mouth spoke, slower than words.

 'You were sent to help the people here.
Their invaders' greatest fear

is that the sky will fall.
Say you'll make this happen
and in two days' time the moon will be eclipsed.'

Awake, he found himself
a crumpled scrap beneath
the upright stack of stone.
Black clouds rolled the moon.

As milkmaid warriors made futile preparations
to defend against attack
their newcomer was welcomed back
with sceptical acclaim.
He told to those who would be told,
then rode
into the enemy domain.

Deriding scowls lined his arrival.
Wolf-eyed soldiers, drunk, with stagnant breath,
press to hear his threat
to make the sky collapse
unless their troops retreat.
The leader's belly heaved, he laughed and spat:
'Before I skewer and feed you to these apes
go tell your tribe, within three days they'll be my slaves.'

Thunder tore apart a sheet of sky.
Hard laughter swallowed dust
as hero sped to anxious settlement.
The villagers made crude defences
huddled in a circle round the stone.
Lambs listened for the dog-pack howl.
Long blown hours scattered charcoal grey

above the rag-bag armies' quickened pulse.
A sudden moon illuminates.
They crouch with bucket, beam and bench
in fortress ring until
night sang,
sang of juggernaut's approach.

'I will make the sky collapse,'
First Person sprang and roared,
'unless you take your army back.'
Some stumbled, stopped,
but most slunk on, shamed
by their leader's mocking curse.

The sky grew black magnetic.
Black air cracked electric.
A drape was dragged across the moon.
In howling darkness some trampled, tripped,
but all ran, chased by children to the laughing sea.

IV

Strings pluck, horns blow, drums beat.
Full-lunged songs sing enemies' defeat.
Sheep set loose, blacksmith's bench returned to use
and milkmaid's buckets spilled with glory tales.
Planted seeds found time to thrive
and farmers rose to reap their ripened wheat.
The warrior, at peace with peace
like thief, resolved to turn a leaf.
And lovers made lovers' plans.
Pebble games, daisy chains
and sub-chin butter tests.

Kids peel sticks of birch to feel
slick moistured fingertips.
Blue sky laced with tight white webs;
fields of high rye tickled skylarks,
levitating stars.

On contented drone of bee
musicians improvise a melody
fuelled by feast fermented fruit.
Sun-cooked air blew through flutes
and round bright maypole strings
a jig in plaited time thrilled quickened hearts.

Birds and butterflies flit
from wayside bush and ditch.
The track from town to stone
soon jammed with revellers
inching chattily towards
their sacred site
where she and he
vowed their proud love.
No kingdom could have crowned him
with more joy than her.

An impossibly distant black bird
circled overhead and wondered why
so many bite-sized creatures spent their lifetime
running on the spot.

VIII Home to Love

Flying to My Home

The sun is fading in the west
Out where the cattle roam,
I'm like a bird at the end of the day
Flying to my home.

I'm flying to my home sweet majesty,
I'm flying to my home.

The sky is like a painted flag
Above a sea of chrome,
I've got a woman living in my life,
Living in my home.

I'm flying to my home sweet majesty,
I'm flying to my home . . .

Full Moon's Eve

On a full moon's eve
A tiger sprang
And gnawed on
Who I used to be

A pale haze lights
The fox's eye
And ...
Checking once
He leaves by a hole in the hedge

Old loves return
To kiss the lips
In case the empty gallery
Should fill with whispering strangers
Like a flood

A Man with Children

I am a man with children
Namely, Heather, Mary, Stella, Sid and James
Well Sid's a lie
But who are you to know
About a fool such as I?

Winds hop and bump
Along the corrugated roof
But here inside
A man of pride
In children

A winter wind was one to blame
For lying us so close
To make each child
And I was told
For each that growed
Their personality would stay
And I'm well proud

The Blue Shines Through

You're responsible
for the hole in my soul
the hole in my tablecloth
the hole in my jacket top
But the hole shines blue
The hole shines blue

I'm responsible
for the bolt in your neck
the bolt from the blue
the bolt on the door
But the blue shines through
the hole in my soul
The blue shines through
The hole shines blue

Calico Skies

It was written that I would love you
From the moment I opened my eyes
And the morning when I first saw you
Gave me life under calico skies
I will hold you for as long as you like
I'll hold you for the rest of my life

Always looking for ways to love you
Never failing to fight at your side
While the angels of love protect us
From the innermost secrets we hide
I'll hold you for as long as you like
I'll hold you for the rest of my life

Long live all of us crazy soldiers
Who were born under calico skies
May we never be called to handle
All the weapons of war we despise
I'll hold you for as long as you like
I'll hold you for the rest of my life
I'll hold you for as long as you like
I'll love you for the rest of my . . .
For the rest of my life

Waterfalls

Don't go jumping waterfalls
Please keep to the lake
People who jump waterfalls
Sometimes can make mistakes

And I need love, yeah I need love
Like a second needs an hour
Like a raindrop needs a shower
Yeah I need love every minute of the day
And it wouldn't be the same
If you ever should decide to go away

And I need love, yeah I need love
Like a castle needs a tower
Like a garden needs a flower
Yeah I need love every minute of the day
And it wouldn't be the same
If you ever should decide to go away

Don't go chasing polar bears
In the great unknown
Some big friendly polar bear
Might want to take you home

And I need love, yeah I need love . . .

Don't run after motor cars
Please stay on the side
Someone's glossy motor car
Might take you for a ride
And I need love, yeah I need love . . .

Don't go jumping waterfalls
Please keep to the lake.

Pictures in Song

Most of her days
She sits waiting for someone
Dreaming of romance
– Some day he'll come along

Most of my life has been spent
Painting pictures in song

He fills his time
Slowly building a home
They can be proud of
Makes it big and strong

I find that I fill my time
Painting pictures in song

Some spend their time
Trying to learn how
To measure the distance
Between right and wrong

Most of my time has been spent
Painting pictures in song

I'll be content
Painting pictures in song

No Rhyme

No rhyme, no reason,
No ship, no shape.
We lie in our long bed
Making escape.

My Love

And when I go away
I know my heart can stay with my love
It's understood
It's in the hands of my love,
And my love does it good.
My love does it good.

And when the cupboard's bare
I'll still find something there with my love
It's understood
It's everywhere with my love,
And my love does it good.
My love does it good.

I love, my love,
Only my love holds the other key to me,
Oh my love, oh my love
Only my love does it good to me.
My love does it good.

Don't ever ask me why
I never say goodbye to my love
It's understood
It's everywhere with my love,
And my love does it good,
My love does it good.

I love my love,
Only my love does it good to me.

Anti-Alarm Call

Don't get up just yet
It's much too cold and wet

Better stay in bed
Hibernate instead

Fifteen minutes more
What you waiting for?
Back into your dreams

Better stay inside
Hibernate and hide

Call It a Day

It's only a matter of hours
Since lurching to left right
Hunched in half light
I dropped from the day night
And sped across fields –

Music for ear drums
Lemon for sore gums
Brambles for bare bums –

Call it a day

Blessed

I would come back from a run
With lines of poetry to tell
And having listened, she would say
'What a mind.'

She'd fold my words inside her head
And though the lines may not have been
Supreme, she wasn't merely being kind.
She meant it, what she said

And I am blessed
For she said 'What a mind.'

Black Jacket

Sadness isn't sadness
it's happiness
in a black jacket

Death isn't death
it's life
that's jumped off a tall cliff

Tears are not tears
They're balls
of laughter
dipped in salt

Her Spirit

Her spirit moves wind chimes
    When air is still
        And fills the rooms
            With fragrance of lily

Her eyes blue green
    Still seen
        Perfectly happy
            With nothing

Her spirit sets
    The water pipes a-humming
        Fat lektronic force be with ya sound

Her spirit talks to me
    Through animals
        Beautiful creature
            Lay with me

Bird that calls my name
    Insists that she is here
        And nothing
            Left to fear

Bright white squirrel
    Foot of tree
        Fixes me
            With innocent gaze

Her spirit talks to me

Meditate

Astride my inner peace
       I see
How many thoughts I throw
       at me

Stem this furious flow of frantic thought

    Meditate

Set aside arrangements to be made
Speeches to be spoken
Pennies on a plate

    Meditate

Listening to glistening bells
Ding dong mantras honey coat a parching thirst
Inner singer shouts out mantra
Drown out lucy nation's chatter

Count for nothing
To count for count's sake
Count
To no total
To repeat
Not to remember, but
To not remember.

To meditate

To listen for nothing
Hear no reason

Mantra discovers
Naughty boy
Inside my mind
Trine to write poetry
Pa-boiled
Mam-marry
Gland opening

Ma shall law declare
Pa takes of the feast

Cunt hooks, quim, minge
Knob and tool
Words I often heard at school
Shall I fear to now repeat
Words that whistled down our street?

Stop

Man tra la la
Man trap

Stop

Mantra mantra

Love sound no meaning

To Find the Joy

Seagulls bright white glint
Against a charcoal morning sky
Enough for lovers to see heaven by
But fox and rabbit badger yeah
And seagull too think harder crueller thoughts –
Do or be done to –
No poet's joy for them

Seagulls spiral whirl
Against the sullen oak
No scientific thought informs
Their common madcap tribal swirl

For them the warming sun
Not only warms but shines
A harsher light to be discovered by
An overshoulder ever-watchful life
While we will quieten our disquiet
    To find the joy

Irish Language

Those Irish chappies
Have a fine sense of it
This language of ours

They toss it in the air
Like a snowball

Dribble it through their fingers
Like the guy in the movie

Tell tales that fell
Off the back of a lorry
Carting logs for the furnace

Swill it round their mouths
And let the spittle drip
Slowly out

Trickle, tumble,
Fiddle, fumble,
Bimble, bumble

To be sure of anything
Would be a fine thing

To be sure
As Spike says –
The Beatles were a bunch of Micks

Steel

Steel yourself against the rapid fire
Confusion of events that masquerade as life
Bullet holes in time's demented curtain

Rocking On!

I want to smell
your underarm odour
I want to drink
your ice cream soda

Reminisce
about our childhood
What we did
in deepest wildwood

Let's remember
fifties cars
And hanging out in
late-night bars

Want to give
your back a rub
Then jump into
a foamy tub

Laugh at all
your High School jokes
One two many
Scotch and Cokes

Want to stroke
your furry kitten
Don't be shy
you won't be bitten

When we've seen
the babies doze off
Let me see you
take your clothes off

When this world is
dead and gone
We will still be
Rocking On!

Dawn Star

You are
the brightest star
in a blue dawn

Venus
above us
between us

we gaze admiringly
like Jupiter

She Is . . .

She is . . .
the Yin to my Yang
the I to my Ching
the See to my Saw
the Head to my Tails
the Lily of my Valley

Lost

I lost my wife
She lost her life

Until then
the luxury
of no responsibility

Chopper wouldn't
fall that night
as, clenched inside a glove
we sucked
each other's energy

To Be Said

There's a lot to be said
There's nothing to be said

My love is alive
My love is dead

I hear her voice
Inside my head

There's a lot to be said
There's nothing to be said

There's a lot to remember
A lot to forget

My love is hot
My love is wet
As if it was
The night we met

There's a lot to remember
A lot to forget

There's a lot to be said
There's nothing to be said

Nova

(from A Garland For Linda)

Are You there?
God where are You?

Are You hiding in Your Heaven?
Or beneath Your deepest sea?
Was there something in our past imperfect?
Or is it something that we should have known?

Are You there?
God where are You?

Are You hiding, God?
Are You hiding in the rain?
Are you hiding?

I am here

I am here in every song you sing
In the wings of a rising lark
Through the darkness to the morning light.
I am present in everything.

I am here as first a new-born babe
Opens eyes on the universe.

I am here
I am here now
I am with you

I am here as every flake of snow
Washes white on the countryside.
As each green blade stretches for the sun.
I am here watching over them.

I am here as first a new-born babe
Opens eyes on the universe.
With each step I'll be that arm that guides
Now and then till the end of time.

     Amen.

Acknowledgements

We would like to thank the following (in alphabetical order) for their help and encouragement: Sherry Baines, Maria Dawson, Alan Durband (Paul's inspirational English teacher), Annabel Hardman, Celia Hewitt, Shelagh Jones, Sasha Mitchell and Tom Pickard. We are both also grateful for the support and enthusiasm shown by the *New Statesman*, which was the original publisher of some of these poems.

Paul McCartney and Adrian Mitchell

Index of Titles

Titles of lyrics are followed by the title of the album on which the song is included.

All Together Now, © Northern Songs, 1968; Back in the USSR, © Northern Songs, 1968; Backwards Traveller, © MPL Communications Ltd, 1978; Band on the Run, © Paul and Linda McCartney, 1974; Big Boys Bickering, © MPL Communications Ltd, 1992; Blackbird, © Northern Songs, 1968; Calico Skies, © MPL Communications Ltd & Inc, 1997; Carry That Weight, © Northern Songs, 1969; Eleanor Rigby, © Northern Songs, 1966; Figure of Eight, © MPL Communications Ltd, 1989; Flaming Pie, © MPL Communications Ltd & Inc, 1997; Flying to My Home, © MPL Communications Ltd, 1989; Golden Earth Girl, © MPL Communications Ltd, 1992, 1993; Heart of the Country, © Northern Songs, 1971; Helen Wheels, © Paul and Linda McCartney, 1974; Here Today, © MPL Communications Ltd, 1982; Hey Jude, © Northern Songs, 1968; Junior's Farm, © Paul and Linda McCartney, 1974; Junk, © Northern Songs, 1970; Lady Madonna, © Northern Songs, 1968; Let 'Em In, © McCartney Music Ltd, 1976; Little Willow, © MPL Communications Ltd & Inc, 1977; Looking for Changes, © MPL Communications Ltd, 1992, 1993; Lovely Rita, © Northern Songs, 1967; Maxwell's Silver Hammer, © Northern Songs, 1969; Maybe I'm Amazed, © Northern Songs, 1970; Monkberry Moon Delight (written with Linda McCartney), © Northern Songs, 1971; Mull of Kintyre, © MPL Communications Ltd, 1977; My Love, © Paul and Linda McCartney, 1973, 1974; Nova, © MPL Communications Ltd, 1999; Ob-la-di, Ob-la-da, © Northern Songs, 1968; Once upon a Long Ago, © MPL Communications Ltd, 1987; Paperback Writer, © Northern Songs, 1966; Penny Lane (written with John Lennon), © Northern Songs, 1967; Picasso's Last Words (Drink to Me), © Paul and Linda McCartney, 1974; Rocky Raccoon, © Northern Songs, 1968; Sergeant Pepper's Lonely Hearts Club Band, © Northern Songs, 1967; She Came in through the Bathroom Window, © Northern Songs, 1969; She's Leaving Home, © Northern Songs, 1967; 'Soily, © MPL Communications Inc, 1976; Standing Stone, © MPL Communications Ltd, 1997; The Fool on the Hill, © Northern Songs, 1967; The Long and Winding Road, © Northern Songs, 1970; The Note You Never Wrote, © McCartney Music Ltd, 1976; The Song We Were Singing, © MPL Communications Ltd & Inc, 1997; The World Tonight, © MPL Communications Ltd & Inc, 1997; Venus and Mars, © McCartney Music Inc, 1975; Waterfalls, © MPL Communications Ltd, 1980; When I'm Sixty-Four, © Northern Songs, 1967; Why Don't We Do It in the Road?, © Northern Songs, 1968; Yellow Submarine, © Northern Songs, 1966; Yesterday, © Northern Songs, 1965. All songs copyright Northern Songs are published by Sony/ATV Music Publishing.